Nature's Children

TOADS

Amanda Harman

GROLIER
EDUCATIONAL

FACTS IN BRIEF

Classification of Toads

Class:	*Amphibia* (amphibians)
Order:	*Anura* (frogs and toads)
Family:	*Bufonidae* (true toads)
Genus:	There are 33 genera of toads.
Species:	There are more than 3,400 species of anurans and around 400 species of true toads.

World distribution.   Worldwide, except Antarctica, the Arctic, Greenland, high mountains, and some oceanic islands.

Habitat.   Damp areas in temperate forests, prairies, swamps, marshes, rain forests, and deserts.

Distinctive physical characteristics.   A large amphibian with rough skin, no tail, short forelegs, and larger hind legs.

Habits.   Toads are nocturnal animals. Most live on land but have to return to water to reproduce.

Diet.   Adults feed mainly on insects, slugs, and earthworms; tadpoles eat algae that they scrape from underwater rocks.

© 1999 Brown Partworks Limited
Printed and bound in U.S.A.
Editor: James Kinchen
Designer: Tim Brown
Reprinted in 2002

Published by:

GROLIER
EDUCATIONAL

Sherman Turnpike, Danbury, Connecticut 06816

Library of Congress Cataloging-in-Publishing Data

Toads.
    p. cm. -- (Nature's children. Set 7)
  ISBN 0-7172-5549-2 (alk. paper) -- ISBN 0-7172-5531-X (set)
  1. Toads--Juvenile Literature. [1. Toads.] I. Grolier Educational (Firm) II. Series.

QL668.E227 T63 2001
597.8'7--dc21

00-067245

Contents

What is the ugliest creature in the animal kingdom? Some people might answer "the warthog," while others might think that a sea slug is even uglier. But for many people the ugliest animal in the world is much closer to home—the toad. The toad is a squat, flabby animal with cold and slimy, or dry and warty, skin, bulging eyes, and a huge, wide mouth. If you can learn to ignore their looks and take the trouble to find out about them though, you will soon learn that there is a lot more to toads than meets the eye.

What do you really know about toads? We all know that toads are closely related to frogs—but what is the difference between them? In fact, is there any difference? Can you catch warts by picking up a toad? How do toads catch their food? And how do some toads protect their eggs and tadpoles from hungry enemies? Read on in this book to discover the answers to all these questions, and to find out about the animal with one of the most amazing tongues in the world!

Wet and Dry

Opposite page:
This common toad from England is just as happy on land as it is swimming in water.

Toads belongs to a group of creatures called the amphibians. This group of animals also includes frogs, caecilians (animals that look a little like worms), newts, and salamanders.

The main thing that amphibians have in common is that they live both on land and in water. For this reason scientists think that amphibians been around on Earth for a very long time. Many scientists think that amphibians are the animals that appeared on Earth after the fish that lived in the sea and before the dinosaurs and reptiles that lived on the land. In frogs and toads the adults generally live on land and breathe air, while the young (called tadpoles) live in ponds and streams. Because they spend all their time underwater, tadpoles have to breathe by filtering water through parts of their body called gills.

Telling the Difference

Toads and frogs are very closely related to each other. They are so closely related that scientists consider them to be the same animals, called anurans. Most people use the names toad and frog to mean those anurans that look a little different from each other, however. Anurans that have smooth, moist skin, live close to water, and leap around using their very long back legs are usually called frogs. Anurans that have rough, warty skin and large bumps behind their eyes are usually called toads. Toads also tend to live in drier places than most frogs and walk clumsily around or make small hops on their short back legs. These differences are not true of all frogs and toads, though. For example, the narrow-mouthed toad hops like a toad but has smooth skin like a frog. In this book we will look only at those anurans that have toad as part of their name.

Opposite page: This is an oak toad. It is the smallest type of toad in America and only grows to be around 1.2 inches (3 centimeters) in length.

9

True Toads

Toads and other frogs have been around on Earth for at least 200 million years. They have not changed very much since the time of the dinosaurs, about 65 million years ago. Now there are around 3,400 species (types). So that they don't get confused by all these different species, scientists divide frogs and toads into 28 different groups called families. Most of these species have the common name of frog, but those in a family called the Bufonidae are called the "true" toads. There are about 400 species in this group. One of the most familiar is the common American toad, which is found in southeastern Canada and throughout the United States.

Today as many as 23 species of toads and frogs are in danger of extinction (dying out), mainly because humans are destroying the forests and wetlands where they live.

A Tale of No Tail

Toads are smallish, squat amphibians. They seem to crouch low down to the ground with their large back legs bent beneath them. Unlike their cousins the salamanders and newts, adult toads and frogs do not have a tail. That is why they have been given the name anurans. It means "tail-less animals."

The smallest toads are just an inch (25 millimeters) long, but the largest toad in the world is the cane toad. Adult males grow to 5.5 inches (14 centimeters) long and just over 2 pounds (1 kilogram) in weight. Adult females are even larger than this—they measure up to 8.5 inches (22 centimeters) in length and weigh as much as 4.5 pounds (1.5 kilograms).

Opposite page: This is a common toad from England. It is one of the larger types of toad and can grow to be up to 4.8 inches (12 centimeters) long.

Warts and Knobs

Opposite page:
This is a South American common toad. Its body shape and coloring make it look just like a dead leaf.

Although some frogs are very brightly colored, toads tend to be quite dull. Their skin is usually covered in spots or blotches that are colored gray, green, brown, and yellow. American toads are reddish-brown with black spots. This blotchy coloration helps camouflage the animals, letting them blend in with their background and avoid being seen by their enemies. Some toads are especially invisible when hiding among fallen leaves on the floor of a forest.

There is a story that you can catch warts by picking up a toad. This is not true at all—no one has ever caught warts from a toad. It is still not a good idea to hold some toads because they have knobby skin that oozes a slightly poisonous substance. This keeps other animals from trying to eat them or people from wanting to pick them up!

Not Island Hoppers

Toads and frogs live almost everywhere in the world, but they are particularly common in the rain forests in the tropics (the tropics are the hot areas that stretch around the Earth just north and south of the equator). Frogs and toads do not live in very cold places such as Antarctica and Greenland. They are also missing from most of the islands in the oceans. That is because they are freshwater animals and die if they are in salty water for too long. Without swimming through the sea, they have no other way of reaching the islands. But on islands where people have taken them, toads and frogs are often able to live very well.

Opposite page:
A young Cameroon toad balances on some mushrooms as it searches the rain forest for food.

Moist Homes

The true toads live in many different places, including forests, prairies, swamps, marshes, tropical rain forests, and even deserts. The American toad prefers moist places along the banks of streams and ponds, in meadows, in forests, and even in backyards. In those areas it shelters under logs and among fallen leaves during the day. Like many other toads and frogs, it takes oxygen in through its skin as well as from the air it breathes into its lungs. Toads can only do this if their skin stays damp.

A Chorus of Toads

Even if you have never seen a toad, you may have heard one at some time. Male American toads can be heard from miles around during the breeding season. It lasts from the end of March to the middle of May. During this time the toads sing or croak loudly. The singing is to attract females to the area so that the males can mate with them. In some toad species the singing also lets other males know a particular area is taken, and they should go somewhere else. Female toads generally do not make any sound at all.

Each kind of toad has its own special type of song. For example, the American toad makes a long trilling sound. The male oak toad sounds like a baby chick chirping, while the narrow-mouthed toad's song sounds like the bleating of a sheep. Species such as the American toad have large sacs in their throat, or at the sides of their mouth, that swell up with air while the toads sing. It makes their songs even louder than they would otherwise be.

Opposite page:
The sac in the throat of this American toad is pumped full of air as it calls.

Big Hugs

Opposite page:
You can see some of the strings of eggs already in the water as these two common toads mate. Some male toads will try to mate with frogs, or even leaves and twigs, until they can find a female toad!

Mating between male and female toads usually takes place in the water. Once he has attracted a female, the male American toad climbs on his partner's back and grasps her with his arms. The males of some species, such as the American toad, have special rough pads on their front feet to allow them to hold on tightly. While the male is still holding on to her, the female lays eggs, which are then fertilized by the male. The fertilized eggs are laid in two sloppy strings, with each egg encased in a see-through gel. Female American toads can lay as many as 12,000 eggs at one time!

Normally, the eggs are left to grow into tadpoles without any further care from the parents. Some toads look after their eggs very carefully, however. There are even toads that do not lay eggs at all but give birth to live tadpoles or toadlets.

Caring Parents

A few European toads are so good at guarding their eggs that they have been given the name midwife toads. A midwife is usually a female nurse who helps a woman give birth. This name is a little misleading for the toad, however, because the parent that does all the caring is not the "wife" at all—it is the "husband"! Once the female has laid her eggs, the male midwife toad fertilizes them and wraps them around his hind legs and back for safety. He then crawls into his burrow, where he can keep the eggs from drying out and also protect them from animals that might try to eat them. The tadpoles hatch from the eggs about a month later.

In the Surinam toad the eggs stick to the female's back after mating. Her skin then begins to grow over the top of the eggs. Two weeks later the eggs hatch, and tiny toads break through their mother's skin. Once free, the toadlets swim away and get no more care from their parents.

Opposite page: A midwife toad with his eggs. Just before the eggs hatch, the male finds a small pool and dangles his legs in the water so the newly hatched tadpoles can swim away.

Wriggly Tadpoles

Opposite page:
These funny looking creatures are tadpoles that will eventually grow up to be common toads.

Unlike human children, who look just like small grownups, young toads look very different from their parents. Tadpoles are small, wriggly water creatures. They do not have a neck separating their head and body— and instead of four legs, they have a thick tail that tapers to a point at the end. This tail has a long fin running down either side of it and is used to push the tadpoles through the water when they swim.

Most tadpoles are vegetarian and feed on algae and dead plant material in the water or on the bottom of the pond. As well as taking in oxygen, a tadpole's gills filter particles from the water. The tadpoles also have special hard "teeth" in their jaws that they use for scraping food from the surface of leaves and stones. Some tadpoles, on the other hand, hunt other tadpoles or insects.

Changing Shape

As the tadpoles grow, they begin to change shape in a process called metamorphosis. It is very similar to the process that happens to insects such as butterflies and beetles, as they grow from wormlike young into winged adults.

Metamorphosis takes around two months in the American toad. During this time the tadpoles slowly become tiny toadlets, growing legs and losing their tails. The tail does not drop off, however—the flesh is taken back inside the body, where the nutrients can be used to help the young toad grow. This process takes much longer in some species and a much shorter time in others. For example, the tadpoles of the North American spadefoot toads change into adults within about two weeks. Adult toads may live for 15 years or so.

Opposite page: You can see the legs just starting to form on these toad tadpoles.

Keeping Warm

Opposite page:
This common toad has just come out of hibernation.

Toads are often described as "cold-blooded." This does not mean that their blood is cold, however. It just means that their body temperature is always the same temperature as the air or water around them. The toad's body has to be kept warm for it to work properly, so toads needs to avoid places where it is cold. Many adult toads do this by hibernating underground throughout the winter. Hibernation is like a very long, deep sleep during which the animal's breathing and heartbeat slow down until they have almost stopped. Hibernation lets the animal survive the long winter because it uses so little energy that the toad does not need to eat until the weather becomes warm again. During their hibernation some toads form a cocoon around themselves for protection. The toads make the cocoon from a sticky liquid that they produce in their bodies. The liquid soon hardens to form a protective coating around the toad.

Drying Out

Opposite page:

When it gets too dry, some toads, like this western green toad from Mexico, hide away until it rains again.

Drying out is a major problem for most types of toad. Without any water at all they would die within about three hours. To keep this from happening, many toads shelter under logs and vegetation or burrow into the ground during the day. This allows them to avoid the heat of the sun and keep cool and moist. These toads are nocturnal, which means they only come out to feed at night.

Many toads are very good at burrowing. The Mexican burrowing toad and the spadefoot toads have tiny spadelike structures on their back feet that they use just for digging. These toads spend most of their life underground and come out of their burrow to breed only after it has been raining heavily. Above its eyes the Asian horned toad has large, pointed ridges, which it uses to dig into soil. One species from Cuba, called the shell-headed toad, even has a head perfectly shaped to act as a lid at the top of its burrow.

Eating Meat

Unlike most tadpoles, adult toads are carnivores (meat-eaters). They live mainly on small animals such as slugs and worms. These animals often have crumbs of soil or tiny stones sticking to them. If you are lucky, you may sometimes see a toad cleaning a worm by holding one end in their mouth and running their front feet along the worm's body.

Toads are unable to chew and have to swallow their food whole. Some species even eat fish, baby birds, and small animals such as mice. One example of such a hungry amphibian is the South American horned toad. The favorite mouthfuls for many toads, however, are insects. One Australian species called the holy cross toad eats nothing but ants. It even lives inside ant nests, so it is always surrounded by its food!

Shooting Tongue

Toads are a little clumsy as they walk around on land and are not able to either outrun or sneak up on their prey (animals that the toads like to eat). Instead, they use their tongue as an amazing hunting weapon! A toad's tongue is attached to the front of its mouth and can flick forward extremely fast. A gooey pad at the end of the tongue sticks to the prey and pulls it back to the toad's mouth for swallowing. Some toads do not catch prey with their tongue. These toads use their mouth to grab their victims from the ground.

Once it has caught its prey, the toad uses its tongue to move the food morsel to the back of its throat and then swallows by blinking. As it closes its eyes, the toad's eyeballs pull inward and force the food down its throat!

Pest Control

American toads are such important hunters of insects that some farmers use them to control insect pests on their crops. Another example of a toad used like this is the cane toad, normally found in Mexico and Central and South America. In the early 20th century humans introduced this creature into Florida, Hawaii, Puerto Rico, New Guinea, and Australia to keep down numbers of pests called sugar cane beetles. This idea did not work in Australia, however. There the cane toad preferred to feed on other insects and left the sugar cane beetles alone. Unfortunately, the cane toad is the largest and one of the most poisonous toads in the world. This means there are not many animals that dare to hunt or eat it. The female also lays up to 35,000 eggs a year. As a result, the number of Australian cane toads kept on increasing, until there were so many that they became serious pests too!

Opposite page: *This is a cane toad. It is the biggest type of toad in the world.*

Seeing and Hearing

Opposite page:
A cane toad peers out from the shelter of a log. Toad's bodies are very good at picking up vibrations from the ground. That helps them know if there are any enemies around.

Toads make a tasty meal for a whole range of carnivores, including foxes, rats, snakes, and birds such as herons and crows. As a result, a toad's senses have to be very good to spot danger whenever it is around. A toad's sight is particularly good, and its large, bulging eyes allow it to see most of its surroundings at once. Unlike you, however, it probably does not see in color. To keep its eyes protected, the toad has see-through eyelids that regularly draw up over the eyeballs.

Toads can also hear very well, which is why they do most of their communicating through sound. These creatures do not have obvious ears, though. Instead, sound is picked up by rings of cartilage in back of the eyes (cartilage is a hard substance a little like bone—the hard parts under the skin of your nose and ears are made from cartilage). The toad's bits of cartilage then send the sound to the inner ears, which are inside the toad's head.

Bluffing

As we have already seen, one way that toads can escape being seen by their enemies is to have colors and patterns on their skin that help them blend in with their surroundings. If they are seen, however, they must make their escape or defend themselves in other ways. Some toads bluff their way out of danger by pretending to be bigger and more aggressive than they really are. They hope that this will scare away their attacker. For example, the American toad stands up on the tips of its toes and blows air into its body to make it look huge and fierce. If this does not work, the toad can hop away, sometimes making small leaps of up to 6 inches (15 centimeters).

Opposite page: *This cane toad is trying to frighten you away by pretending to be much bigger and fiercer than he really is.*

Poisonous Skin

Opposite page:
It is easy to see how fire-bellied toads such as this one got their name.

The best defense of all for a toad is to have bad tasting or poisonous skin, so that other animals will not want to eat them. Many species have glands on their back and their head that ooze slimy poison. To advertise this fact and warn hungry hunters to keep away, some species have bright colors and striking patterns on their skin.

The fire-bellied toad gets its name because its underside is covered with a bright yellow-and-black pattern. The belly is normally hidden from view; but whenever the toad feels that it is threatened, it throws itself down onto its back and shows its warning colors. Other animals recognize this sign and do not try to pick up the toad.

Squirting Venom

Most toad poisons are not very strong but taste disgusting to animals that try to eat them. Others, such as the Colorado River toad, are highly poisonous and can kill an animal as large as a dog if it picks the toad up in its mouth. Some toads do not have to wait for an animal to pick them up to use their poison. The cane toad, for example, has huge, puffed-up poison glands on either side of its neck. It can use them to squirt venom (poison) at an enemy over 3 feet (1 meter) away!

Some animals, such as herons, will eat only healthy, living animals, while others are able to see and catch creatures only if they are moving. A European species—the natterjack toad—takes advantage of these facts by lying still and pretending to be dead whenever a heron or other hunter approaches.

Words to Know

Amphibian An animal that lives both on land and in water.

Anuran The group of "tail-less" amphibians that includes the toads.

Breed To produce young.

Camouflage Patterns or colors that help an animal blend in with its surroundings.

Carnivore An animal that eats meat.

Cartilage A type of tissue that is a little like bone, but not as hard, and is more flexible.

Cold-blooded When an animal's body temperature depends on the temperature of its surroundings.

Extinct When all the animals of a particular species have died, and there are no more left anywhere in the world.

Fertilize The joining of sperm from the male and eggs from the female to create an egg that can grow into a baby.

Gill A tadpole's "nostrils"—the flaps through which they suck water in order to get the oxygen they need to live.

Hibernate To go into a very deep "sleep" for the winter.

Mate To come together to produce young.

Metamorphosis The big changes that an animal goes through as it grows from an egg into an adult.

INDEX

Cover Photo: Stephen Dalton / NHPA
Photo Credits: T. Kitchin & V. Hurst / NHPA, page 4; David Woodfall / NHPA, page 7; James Carmichael Jr. / NHPA, page 8; M. P. L. Fogden / Bruce Coleman, page 11; Hans Reinhard / Bruce Coleman, page 12; Kevin Schafer / NHPA, page 15; Gilles Nicolet / Still Pictures, page 16; Stephen Dalton / NHPA, pages 19, 23, 36; Robert Erwin / NHPA, page 20; Daniel Heuclin / NHPA, page 24; G. I. Bernard / NHPA, page 27; Kim Taylor / Bruce Coleman, page 28; Andrew Purcell / Bruce Coleman, page 31; Karl Switak / NHPA, page 33; Pavel German / NHPA, page 38; Joe McDonald / Bruce Coleman, pages 41, 45; A.N.T. / NHPA, page 42.